THE
POPE

Paul Harrison

WAYLAND

First published in 2014 by Wayland
Copyright © Wayland 2014

Wayland
338 Euston Road
London NW1 3BH

Wayland Australia
Level 17/207 Kent Street
Sydney, NSW 2000

Editor: Elizabeth Brent
Designer: Elaine Wilkinson

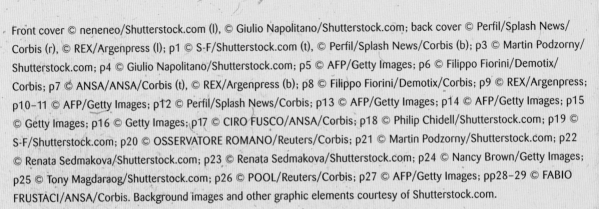

Front cover © neneneo/Shutterstock.com (l), © Giulio Napolitano/Shutterstock.com; back cover © Perfil/Splash News/ Corbis (r), © REX/Argenpress (l); p1 © S-F/Shutterstock.com (t), © Perfil/Splash News/Corbis (b); p3 © Martin Podzorny/ Shutterstock.com; p4 © Giulio Napolitano/Shutterstock.com; p5 © AFP/Getty Images; p6 © Filippo Fiorini/Demotix/ Corbis; p7 © ANSA/ANSA/Corbis (t), © REX/Argenpress (b); p8 © Filippo Fiorini/Demotix/Corbis; p9 © REX/Argenpress; p10–11 © AFP/Getty Images; p12 © Perfil/Splash News/Corbis; p13 © AFP/Getty Images; p14 © AFP/Getty Images; p15 © Getty Images; p16 © Getty Images; p17 © CIRO FUSCO/ANSA/Corbis; p18 © Philip Chidell/Shutterstock.com; p19 © S-F/Shutterstock.com; p20 © OSSERVATORE ROMANO/Reuters/Corbis; p21 © Martin Podzorny/Shutterstock.com; p22 © Renata Sedmakova/Shutterstock.com; p23 © Renata Sedmakova/Shutterstock.com; p24 © Nancy Brown/Getty Images; p25 © Tony Magdaraog/Shutterstock.com; p26 © POOL/Reuters/Corbis; p27 © AFP/Getty Images; pp28–29 © FABIO FRUSTACI/ANSA/Corbis. Background images and other graphic elements courtesy of Shutterstock.com.

A cataloguing record for this title is available at the British Library.

ISBN 978 0 7502 8326 7

Ebook ISBN 978 0 7502 8775 3

Dewey Number 282'.092-dc23

Printed in China

10 9 8 7 6 5 4 3 2 1

Wayland is a division of Hachette Children's Books, an Hachette UK company
www.hachette.co.uk

CONTENTS

A NEW POPE

The news raced around the world. It was 11 February 2013 and Pope Benedict XVI, the head of the Catholic Church, had announced that he was resigning.

This was a headline-grabbing story. Only one pope had ever resigned before and that was nearly 600 years before, when Pope Gregory VI stood down in 1415. Normally the Pope stayed in the job until he died; but Benedict had decided that he was too ill and frail to continue. He felt that the responsibility of leading more than one billion Catholics was too much for him, and he was stepping aside.

▶ Cardinal Bergoglio lived in Buenos Aires in Argentina.

WHO NEXT?

When the news of Benedict's decision broke, there was a lot of discussion about why he had made his choice, what his legacy would be and where he would go next. However, there was an even bigger question that needed answering: who would be the new pope? Few people guessed correctly.

CARDINAL BERGOGLIO

The man chosen was Cardinal Jorge Bergoglio from Argentina – the first Latin American to be made pope. In keeping with tradition, he had taken a new name on becoming pope; he chose Francis, after Saint Francis of Assisi. This was another first – no other pope had taken that name before. Beyond these few facts, not many people knew much about him. Who was Jorge Bergoglio? What was his background? What did he stand for? What sort of pope would he be? The world was about to find out.

◀ Pope Benedict was 85 years old when he chose to resign.

Jorge Bergoglio was born in Argentina, but his father was actually Italian, and had emigrated to South America in 1929.

Mario Bergoglio, Jorge's father, had decided to leave Italy because he disagreed with the politics of the Italian leader at that time, the fascist dictator Benito Mussolini. Some of Mario's family had already moved to Argentina, a country that welcomed immigrants, and Mario wanted to join them. Jorge's mother, Regina Sivori, was Argentinian, as was her father, but her mother was originally from Italy. Regina and Mario met at a church function in a place called Almagro in 1934, and they were married a year later. Jorge was their first child and he was soon followed by four siblings – two brothers and two sisters.

Name: Jorge Mario Bergoglio

Born: Buenos Aires, Argentina

Date of Birth: 17 December 1936

Parents: Mario Giuseppe Francesco Bergoglio (father), Regina Maria Sivori (mother)

Brothers: Oscar Adrian, Alberto Horacio

Sisters: Marta Regina, Maria Elena

Jobs: Cleaner, office worker, bouncer, lab technician, teacher

Favourite pastimes: Dancing, opera, football

Favourite football team: San Lorenzo de Amalgro

WORKING HARD

Mario had come to Argentina to better himself and he believed he would achieve this by hard work. It was a lesson he was keen to pass on to his children, so when Jorge was thirteen years old his father sent him out to work as a cleaner – even though he was still at school. Jorge still did well academically, however, and the money he earned helped the family – and gave him a little to spend himself. It also taught him the value of hard work, and what people had to do to get by.

▶ Jorge's mother's family. Regina stands at the back in the middle.

JUGGLING JOBS

Once he had left school, Jorge went on to study chemistry at college. He continued to work alongside his studies, taking various different jobs. For a while he was a bouncer at a nightclub; he also worked in an office and then became a technician in a laboratory. It was tough; he would start work at seven in the morning, work until one and then go to college. His lectures would last until eight o'clock in the evening, and then it would be home to eat and sleep before it all began again the next day. But Jorge was keen to do well and to work hard, so he stuck at his task.

◀ Regina and Mario Bergoglio on their wedding day.

GOD CALLING

Even though Jorge was busy with college and work he still found time for a social life.

In September 1953, he arranged to meet his friends and his girlfriend one weekend for a picnic. Jorge was now 17 years old, and planning to use the day out to propose to his girlfriend. It did turn out to be a day to remember, but not in the way he had been expecting. Waiting for the train that would take him to the picnic, Jorge had some time to spare and decided to visit a nearby church. While he was there he spoke to the priest. During their conversation, he felt something change inside him; he said later it was as though God had come looking for him.

▲ Jorge at school (third from left, second row up).

◀ The seminary Jorge entered to study to become a priest.

He realized that he didn't want to get married – he wanted to be a priest instead. Jorge didn't meet his friends that day, nor did he propose. Instead he went home to think about what he should do.

FALLING ILL

Choosing to become a priest was a big step and Jorge put off the decision for four years; but eventually he made up his mind not to ignore God any longer. Then disaster struck: Jorge fell ill, was diagnosed with pneumonia and had part of his right lung removed. For three days after the operation it was touch and go whether he would survive – but thankfully he pulled through.

BECOMING A PRIEST

When Jorge was 21, he finally told his parents he wanted to be a priest. His mother was not happy; the news took her by surprise and she wanted her son to finish college first. But Jorge's mind was made up, so he joined a Jesuit seminary to start his training. While at the seminary he worked as a teacher at Jesuit-run colleges in Santa Fe and Buenos Aires, teaching literature and psychology. Eventually, in 1969, after twelve years of training and teaching, Jorge was ordained as a priest. He was now Father Bergoglio, and his new life had truly begun.

Who are the Jesuits?

During his training, Jorge joined a religious order called the Jesuits. Their real name is the Society of Jesus and they were formed in 1540 by a Spanish priest called Ignatius of Loyola (now known as Saint Ignatius). Like all priests they take vows of poverty, chastity and obedience. However, the Jesuits also make a vow of obedience to the Pope, so the Pope can send them where he feels necessary. Traditionally, the Jesuits are sent on missions or to work in education.

TROUBLED TIMES

For much of the time that Jorge was living in Argentina, the country was run by the military.

From the 1930s onwards, the government was overthrown by the armed forces a number of times, in what is called a coup. There were long periods of unrest and, following a coup in the 1970s, Argentina was plunged into one of the darkest periods in its history. The military government began torturing and murdering people who disagreed with them. More than 30,000 Argentinians 'disappeared' – abducted by the government and either imprisoned without trial, or murdered.

As a priest and then a bishop during these difficult times, Jorge saw some of these terrible crimes for himself. Early in Jorge's papacy, there was a storm of controversy when it was claimed that he had worked with the military government – betraying two priests who were then imprisoned and tortured. However, these allegations were disproven when one of the priests in question spoke out against them. In fact, it appears that Jorge actually helped people to escape from the government's clutches, rather than the other way round, by letting people hide on Church property. One person even escaped the country using Jorge's identity papers!

The Dirty War

The grim period in Argentina's history from the 1970s to 1983 when the government's opponents were imprisoned, tortured or murdered has become known as the Dirty War. Although people rioted against the regime, the Dirty War came to an end only in 1982 when Argentina lost a real war with Britain over the Falkland Islands. This defeat led to the downfall of the government, too. Forced into elections, they were voted out and Argentina returned to real democracy.

▼ Soldiers on the streets of Buenos Aires during a coup.

BECOMING A CARDINAL

Right to the top

There are many different ranks and jobs within the Catholic Church, but these are the main ones, in order of seniority:

Deacon – a deacon assists a parish priest, and is often a trainee priest themselves.

Priest – a priest is usually in charge of a parish, a community centred around a church.

Bishop – a bishop oversees a number of parishes called a diocese.

Archbishop – an archbishop is in charge of a number of dioceses.

Cardinal – often the highest ranking member of the Church in a particular country, although some cardinals are not attached to an individual country.

Pope – the head of the Catholic Church.

Father Bergoglio's studies did not end with his ordination.

In 1970, he was sent to join the Jesuit community in Spain, returning to Argentina in 1971 to take up a post in charge of training priests at a seminary in San Miguel. All the while, he also worked towards getting an advanced degree, called a doctorate, in theology.

RISING THROUGH THE RANKS

It wasn't just Jorge's education that was advancing – he was promoted to more and more important jobs within the Church. In 1973, he was made Provincial Superior of Argentina and Uruguay – the highest-ranking member of the Jesuits in these countries. In 1992, he was made auxiliary, or assistant, bishop of Buenos Aires, then nearly six years later, in 1998, he became the archbishop. Finally, in 2001, Jorge was made a cardinal – becoming the most important Catholic priest in Argentina.

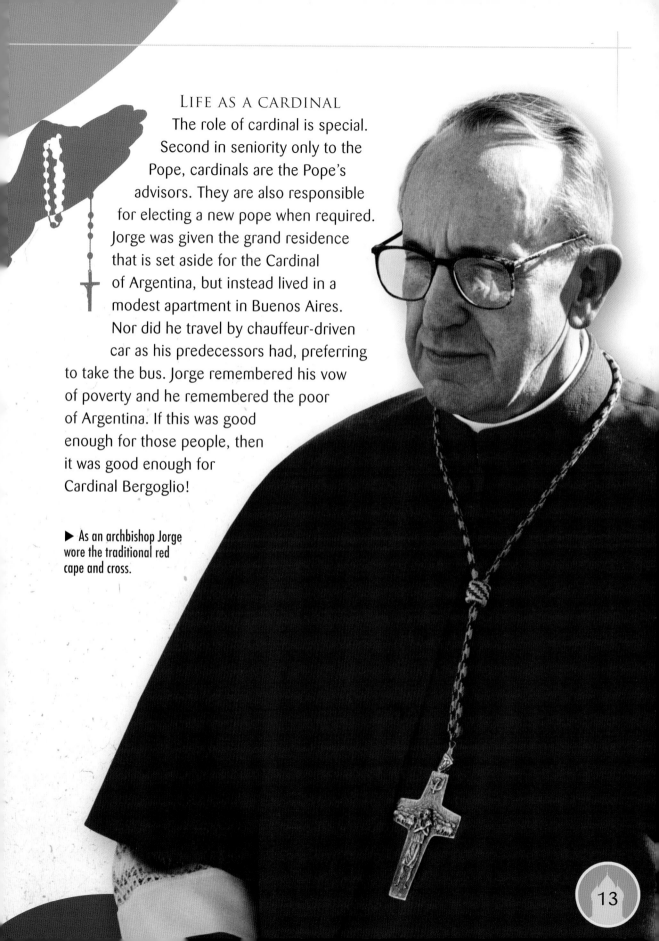

LIFE AS A CARDINAL

The role of cardinal is special. Second in seniority only to the Pope, cardinals are the Pope's advisors. They are also responsible for electing a new pope when required. Jorge was given the grand residence that is set aside for the Cardinal of Argentina, but instead lived in a modest apartment in Buenos Aires. Nor did he travel by chauffeur-driven car as his predecessors had, preferring to take the bus. Jorge remembered his vow of poverty and he remembered the poor of Argentina. If this was good enough for those people, then it was good enough for Cardinal Bergoglio!

▶ As an archbishop Jorge wore the traditional red cape and cross.

TO ROME

When the news came of Pope Benedict's abdication, for Cardinal Bergoglio, and more than 100 fellow cardinals, it meant organizing a trip to Rome.

All the cardinals below 80 years of age had to vote for the new pope. Cardinal Bergoglio had done this before, in 2005, when Pope Benedict was elected. Then, Bergoglio had come second in the elections, but this time, no one thought he would win. At nearly 77 years old, he was thought too old to become pope.

INTERREGNUM

The period of time without a pope is known as an interregnum. The cardinals are called to Rome and must make their way to Vatican City, home of the Catholic Church, within two weeks for a meeting called the conclave. The election that follows is a highly secretive affair. The cardinals are locked into the Sistine Chapel, the famous church within the Vatican, and must

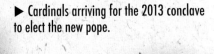

▶ Cardinals arriving for the 2013 conclave to elect the new pope.

▶ The crowds wait expectantly in St Peter's Square.

stay there until they have chosen a new pope. At night they are allowed to stay in secure lodging, but no news of their voting must leak out.

THE CONCLAVE

During the conclave, the cardinals pray and cast their votes in secret at set times. If one cardinal attracts two thirds of the votes plus one, then he is elected pope. Normally this process takes a few days, but it has been known to take years! This time, though, a decision was reached just five rounds of voting later, barely 24 hours after the conclave began. The crowds gathered in St Peter's Square, outside the Vatican, saw white smoke pouring from the chimney of the Sistine Chapel – the official sign a pope had been elected. But no one outside the conclave yet knew that it was Cardinal Bergoglio.

Holy smoke

The only way the rest of the world knows what's going on inside the Sistine Chapel is by the colour of the smoke coming from the chimney. After each round of voting, the papers the cardinals vote with are burnt. Chemicals are added to the flames to give them a distinct colour: black smoke means no one has been elected; white smoke means there is a new pope.

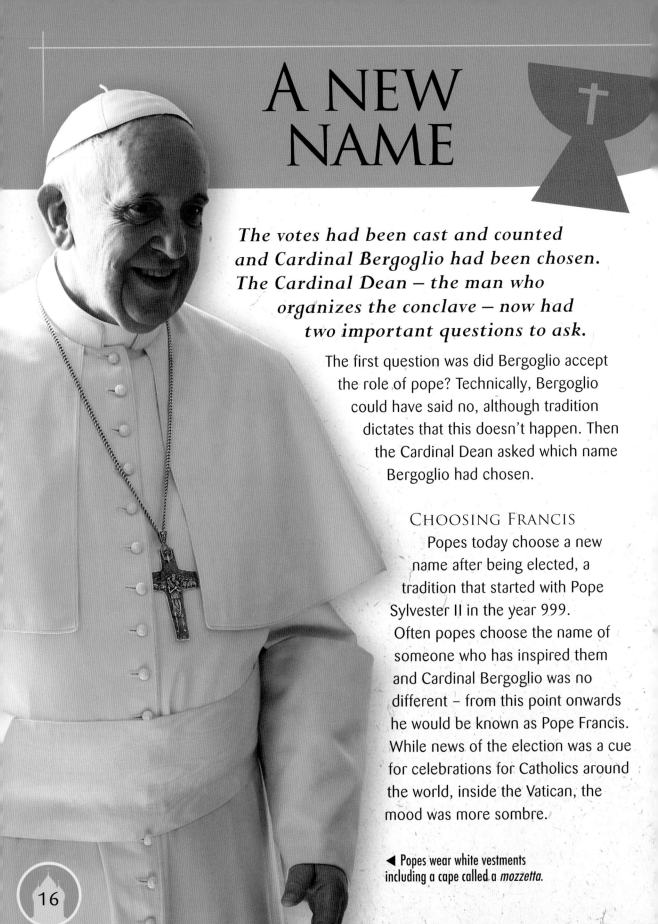

A NEW NAME

The votes had been cast and counted and Cardinal Bergoglio had been chosen. The Cardinal Dean – the man who organizes the conclave – now had two important questions to ask.

The first question was did Bergoglio accept the role of pope? Technically, Bergoglio could have said no, although tradition dictates that this doesn't happen. Then the Cardinal Dean asked which name Bergoglio had chosen.

CHOOSING FRANCIS

Popes today choose a new name after being elected, a tradition that started with Pope Sylvester II in the year 999.

Often popes choose the name of someone who has inspired them and Cardinal Bergoglio was no different – from this point onwards he would be known as Pope Francis. While news of the election was a cue for celebrations for Catholics around the world, inside the Vatican, the mood was more sombre.

◀ Popes wear white vestments including a cape called a *mozzetta*.

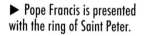

▶ Pope Francis is presented with the ring of Saint Peter.

NEW CLOTHES

The new Pope Francis was taken to a small room known as the 'room of tears', so-called because new popes are often overcome with emotion when they realize the weight of responsibility that now rests on their shoulders. In this room Pope Francis put on his new white robes – the clothes he would wear from then on. He also put on the white sash and skull cap (called a *zucchetto*) that waited for him, but did not take the new red shoes, preferring to keep his old ones. After dressing, Pope Francis was presented again to the cardinals and given his ring of Saint Peter, also known as the Fisherman's Ring. This is the symbol of his authority. It is inscribed with his name on the inside, and Francis will wear it until he stops being pope, when the ring will be destroyed.

Who was Saint Francis?

Saint Francis of Assisi lived in Italy from around 1181 to 1226, and is known for setting up a religious order of monks called the Franciscans. He and his followers took a vow of poverty and lived a very simple life. Saint Francis is the patron saint of small animals.

17

BUSINESS AS USUAL

Jorge Bergoglio was now pope. The Argentinian son of immigrant parents – and the first South American to be elected pope – was now leader of the biggest branch of Christianity in the world.

His office was the Vatican City, his home was the sumptuous papal apartments, he had a golden throne and a special, bulletproof car nicknamed the 'Popemobile' to drive him everywhere. This was not the world Jorge Bergoglio had known when he was growing up; nor was it the world Father Bergoglio, or even Cardinal Bergoglio, had known in Buenos Aires before that life-changing day in Rome.

A NEW WAY OF DOING THINGS

Now Pope Francis didn't see why it had to be that way after becoming pope, either. Immediately after his election, Francis turned down the offer of a private car, and took the

▼ People flock around Francis as he drives past in the Popemobile.

same bus as the other cardinals back to the hotel where they had been staying before the conclave. There he paid for his room, then took the bus to Saint Martha's House, a guest-house in the Vatican. He decided he would stay here, rather than the lavish home previous popes had taken in the Vatican.

A DIFFERENT POPE

Francis had found a way of living that kept him closer to God, and he didn't want to alter it now – to him it was more important than ever to keep his way of life going. This probably came as a bit of a shock to some, but few would have guessed how these actions would signify a very different type of pope.

Holy city

Although it sits within the Italian capital city of Rome, Vatican City is actually the world's smallest independent state. This means it has its own government – in this case headed by the Pope – and an army, called the Swiss Guard. The city is roughly 0.44 kilometres square (0.2 square miles) in size and has a population of around 800 people.

A MODERN POPE

Vatican City can be an imposing place to visit. The main church, St Peter's Basilica, is enormous, and approached across a huge open plaza called St Peter's Square.

Thousands of visitors flock there to try and catch a glimpse of the Pope during his weekly appearances, called audiences. Other tourists queue to visit the Sistine Chapel, which has a world-famous ceiling painted by the Italian master Michelangelo, who also designed and built the huge dome over the basilica. It all looks and feels very grand. But now, overseeing it all, is frugal Pope Francis.

LEADING BY EXAMPLE

Francis has said he wants 'a poor church for the poor'. He is keen to show that the Church isn't about lavish buildings, but about the people who come to worship God. It is about the way these people live their lives, and about reaching out to people who may feel unwanted by the Church or by society. Francis intends to lead by example. On his first Holy Thursday, one of the most important dates in the Catholic calendar, as pope, Francis said Mass as he was expected to. However, rather than using St Peter's Basilica as is usual, Francis went to a young offenders institute, where juvenile prisoners are held. Francis reasoned that the prisoners couldn't come to him, so he would go to them.

◀ Francis washes the feet of young offenders in a show of humility.

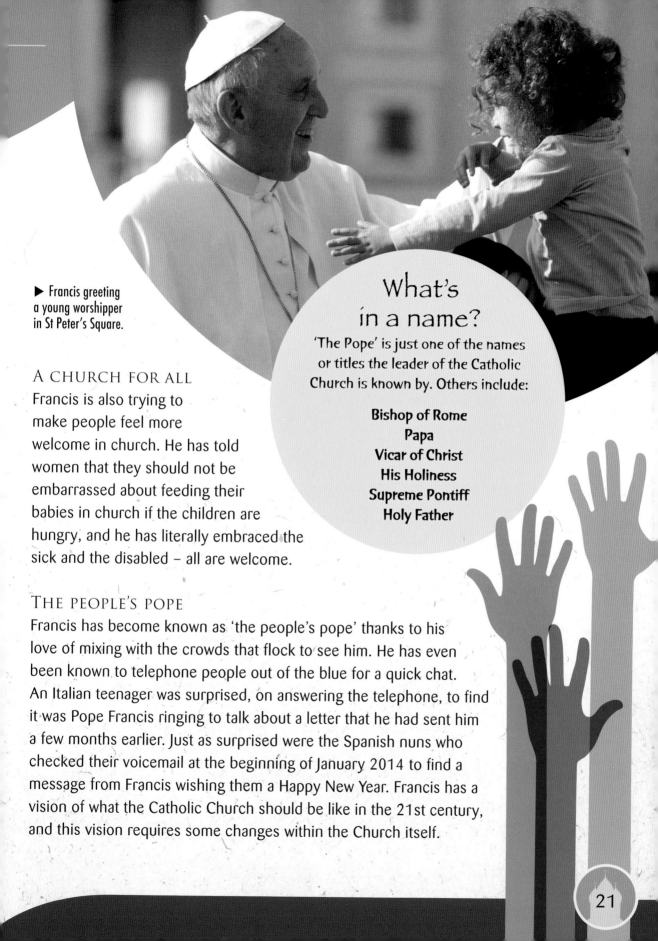

► Francis greeting
a young worshipper
in St Peter's Square.

A CHURCH FOR ALL

Francis is also trying to
make people feel more
welcome in church. He has told
women that they should not be
embarrassed about feeding their
babies in church if the children are
hungry, and he has literally embraced the
sick and the disabled – all are welcome.

What's in a name?

'The Pope' is just one of the names
or titles the leader of the Catholic
Church is known by. Others include:

**Bishop of Rome
Papa
Vicar of Christ
His Holiness
Supreme Pontiff
Holy Father**

THE PEOPLE'S POPE

Francis has become known as 'the people's pope' thanks to his
love of mixing with the crowds that flock to see him. He has even
been known to telephone people out of the blue for a quick chat.
An Italian teenager was surprised, on answering the telephone, to find
it was Pope Francis ringing to talk about a letter that he had sent him
a few months earlier. Just as surprised were the Spanish nuns who
checked their voicemail at the beginning of January 2014 to find a
message from Francis wishing them a Happy New Year. Francis has a
vision of what the Catholic Church should be like in the 21st century,
and this vision requires some changes within the Church itself.

THE CATHOLIC CHURCH

As pope, Francis is the head of the Catholic Church, and leads over one billion followers worldwide. Catholics trace their religion back to the followers of Jesus, called the apostles.

Like all Christians, Catholics believe that Jesus sent his apostles to spread his message and teachings. Unlike other Christian religions, however, Catholics regard the apostle Peter as their first leader. That means Francis is the latest in a long line of popes stretching back nearly 2,000 years. Catholics believe, as do other Christians, that Jesus was the son of God who died on a cross, rose again and a while later ascended into heaven. They believe that there is a life in heaven after death and that you should live your life by a certain set of social and spiritual rules. Catholics also pray to Jesus' mother, Mary, as an intermediary.

◀ Jesus had twelve followers who we call the apostles.

▶ The flames represent
God inspiring the first Christians.

REFORMING THE CHURCH

The Church has found itself criticized
over its stance on topics such as
abortion and contraception (neither of
which it allows), homosexuality, its ban on female
priests, divorce, priests being forbidden to marry, instances
of abuse of children, and financial irregularities. On issues such as
married priests, female priests and contraception, Francis believes
in the existing teachings of the Church, so has no plans for these to
change. However he knows there are other, much-needed, reforms to
be made and he has wasted little time in getting started.

The first Pope

Saint Peter was one of Jesus' first
apostles. He was a fisherman, but gave this
up immediately when Jesus called him. At that
point Peter was called Simon, but Jesus changed
his name to Peter, which means 'rock'. Jesus told
him he would be the rock on which the Church
was built. After Jesus ascended into heaven,
Peter preached about him and is said to have
performed miracles. He attracted lots of
followers and, according to tradition, travelled
to Rome where he was executed because of
his religion, like many early Christians. It is
thought that bones found buried under
the high altar of St Peter's Basilica
belong to him.

TIME TO CHANGE

Pope Francis knew he needed to make sure the Church was organized properly before he could begin to get his message across about how it should work.

This meant making changes that had the potential to be unpopular with his fellow clergy. One of the first things he did on becoming pope was to set about reforming the Curia, the body that is in charge of the day-to-day running of the Church.

THE CURIA

An organization as big as the Catholic Church requires a lot of administrative work. This is the role of the Curia, but it has attracted criticism from people who feel it acts as though the Church is there to support it, rather than the other way round. Francis appointed eight cardinals to investigate the way the Curia works and to overhaul it. He also appointed a new cardinal to take charge of Vatican finances.

THE VATICAN BANK

Another organization that needed attention was the Vatican's bank,

◄ Catholic Masses can be very grand and traditional celebrations.

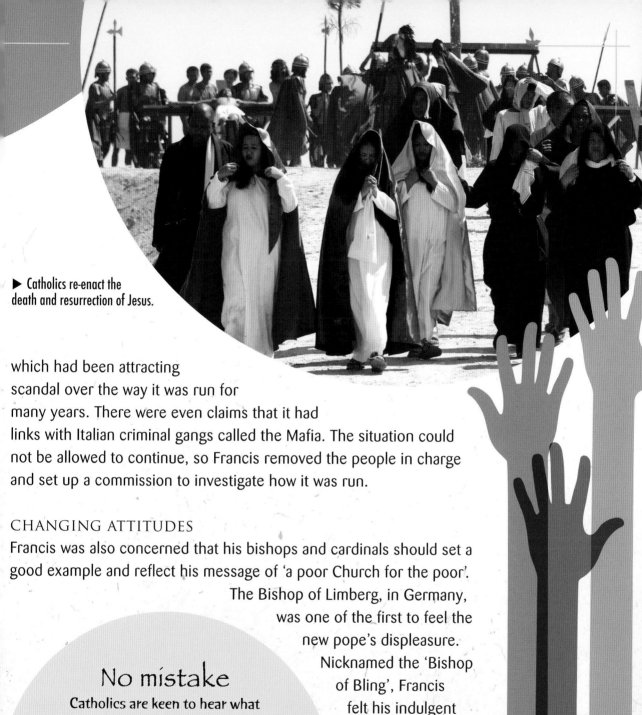

▶ Catholics re-enact the death and resurrection of Jesus.

which had been attracting scandal over the way it was run for many years. There were even claims that it had links with Italian criminal gangs called the Mafia. The situation could not be allowed to continue, so Francis removed the people in charge and set up a commission to investigate how it was run.

CHANGING ATTITUDES

Francis was also concerned that his bishops and cardinals should set a good example and reflect his message of 'a poor Church for the poor'. The Bishop of Limberg, in Germany, was one of the first to feel the new pope's displeasure. Nicknamed the 'Bishop of Bling', Francis felt his indulgent lifestyle was inappropriate for a bishop, and removed him from his post.

No mistake

Catholics are keen to hear what Pope Francis says on various topics, because his word is law. Whenever the Pope speaks officially about Church teaching or morals, these pronouncements are said to be without error, or infallible. This is called Papal Infallibility and has been Church Law since 1870. Such pronouncements are rare, but important because they affect the way Catholics follow their faith and live their lives.

A GLOBAL DIALOGUE

The Catholic Church may have over one billion followers, but it is just one of many different religions globally.

Some of these religions, such as some parts of the Church of England, are very similar to the Catholic faith. Other religions are very different. Religious differences have been a cause for conflict throughout history and this is still the case today. Francis is very aware of the need to build strong relationships with the other world religions.

BUILDING BRIDGES

Fortunately, Francis has a good track record of meeting with and talking to other religious leaders. Before becoming pope, Francis was praised for his work with and

▶ Pope Francis with Tawadros II, leader of the Coptic Orthodox Church.

▶ Francis meets the Israeli Prime Minister Benjamin Netanyahu.

respect for the Jewish, Muslim and Eastern Orthodox religions, and he continues that work in his new role. Francis has talked of the need for different religions to respect and understand each other, and has stressed the similarities between the major religions, rather than the differences.

INTER-FAITH MEETINGS

Francis has also met with religious leaders from many different faiths. He invited a group representing Jewish Americans to meet him, and spoke to them about the need for cooperation. Another visitor to the Vatican was the General Secretary of the Organization of Islamic Cooperation, an influential Islamic group. The General Secretary left the meeting impressed with Francis' determination to strengthen the bond and understanding between the two religions. Francis addressed Muslims directly in a speech to mark the end of Ramadan, their month of fasting. He said:

> We all know that mutual respect is fundamental in any human relationship, especially among people who express a religious belief. In this way, sincere and lasting friendship can grow.

LOOKING TO THE FUTURE

Looking to the future, Pope Francis continues to search for ways to continue his mission and spread his message about caring for one another and including everyone.

At a recent meeting of the World Economic Forum – an organization that brings together political leaders, influential businessmen and invited speakers – Francis told them it was wrong that people in the world were starving when so much food goes to waste. He challenged them to remember their responsibilities to the weak and vulnerable, and to make economic decisions for everyone's benefit.

LISTENING TO THE PEOPLE

Francis knows that respecting one another also means listening to each other, too. In an unprecedented move, he has set up a

◀ Crowds gather to be blessed by Francis.

questionnaire for Catholics around the world to answer. It includes questions on family life and issues such as same sex marriage. Francis hopes that the responses will show him how ordinary people feel about their faith.

THE 'FRANCIS EFFECT'

The appointment of Pope Francis has proved to be a good decision: attendance figures at Catholic Masses are rising, something the media puts down to the 'Francis effect'. Francis enjoys a positive profile in the world's newspapers and magazines, too. In 2013, the American magazine *Time* made him their person of the year – an honour they bestow annually on the person whom they believe to have made the biggest impact in the world that year. However, Francis' greatest achievement by far is the positivity he has given Catholics about their faith. In recent times, the Church has appeared to be struggling, both with internal difficulties and structural problems, and with its perception globally. Yet under Francis' leadership, it seems to be looking to the future with a renewed sense of purpose that bodes well for a stronger, more united Church moving forwards.

"We need to avoid the spiritual sickness of a church that is wrapped up in its own world: when a church becomes like this it grows sick. It is true that going out on to the street implies the risks of accidents happening, as they would to any ordinary man or woman. But if the Church stays wrapped up in itself, it will age. And if I had to choose between a wounded church that goes out onto the streets and a sick withdrawn church, I would definitely choose the first one."

▶ Pope Francis blessing his followers at a service in Rome during Holy Week.

GLOSSARY

Abducted taken away, or kidnapped

Abortion the deliberate ending of a pregnancy during the early months

Administrative of the management of an organization

Apostle one of the followers and companions of Jesus

Chastity abstaining from sexual intercourse

Christian someone who believes in the teachings of Jesus

Clergy people trained to work in the church, such as priests, bishops and cardinals

Contraception methods of avoiding pregnancy

Controversy a public dispute or argument over an issue

Dictator a ruler with complete and overall power

Divorce when a married couple are no longer married according to the law

Eastern Orthodox a branch of the Christian religion

Immigrants people from a foreign country who move to a new country to live

Jewish from the religion of Judaism

Mass a type of religious service

Muslims followers of the Islamic religion

Pneumonia a type of serious lung disease

Questionnaire a series of questions on a subject

Ramadan the ninth lunar month of the Islamic calendar, a holy month marked by fasting between sunrise and sunset

Reforms changes

Seminary a school or college for priests

Theology the study of God and religion

Tradition beliefs and customs passed down through history

Vatican both the city within Rome where the Pope lives and the government of the Catholic Church

Vestments robes worn by the clergy

Vulnerable at risk

Further information

Websites

http://www.vatican.va/phome_en.htm
http://poy.time.com/2013/12/11/person-of-the-year-pope-francis-the-peoples-pope/
http://www.bbc.co.uk/news/world-21701046

Books

Pope Francis in his Own Words, Schwietert Collazo J. and Rogak L., William Collins 2013

Pope Francis: Conversations with Jorge Bergoglio, Rubin S. and Ambrogetti F., Hodder and Stoughton 2013

Francis: Bishop of Rome, Collins M., Columba Press 2013

Places to Visit

Vatican City, Rome, Italy

INDEX